Arts: A Third Level Course
The Nineteenth-century Novel and its Legacy   Unit 31

James Joyce

Prepared by Graham Martin
for the Course Team

The Open University Press

COVER ILLUSTRATION:

Joyce aged 22 in 1904. Asked what he was thinking when C. P. Curran photographed him, Joyce replied, 'I was wondering would he lend me five shillings. '(National Library of Ireland. Photo: C. P. Curran)

The Open University Press
Walton Hall Milton Keynes

First published 1973.

Designed by the Media Development Group of the Open University.

Printed in Great Britain by
Martin Cadbury Printing Group, a division of Santype International.

ISBN 0 335 00831 3

This text forms part of an Open University course. The complete list of units in the course appears at the end of this text.

For general availability of supporting material referred to in this text, please write to the Director of Marketing, The Open University, P.O. Box 81, Walton Hall, Milton Keynes, MK7 6AA.

Further information on Open University courses may be obtained from the Admissions Office, The Open University, P O. Box 48, Walton Hall, Milton Keynes, MK7 6AA.

CONTENTS

Introduction

This unit has four principal aims.

1 To give you some idea of the individual flavour of Joyce's work from the study of one or two texts.

2 To suggest the scope and range of his whole achievement.

3 To underline the element of formal experiment in his artistic career.

4 To suggest ways in which his work throws retrospective light on the nineteenth-century novel.

The set text is *The Essential James Joyce* (ed. Harry Levin), Penguin, 1963. The set reading is 'Eveline', and 'The Dead', from the collection of short stories called *Dubliners*; Chapter One from *The Portrait of the Artist as a Young Man*; and the section called 'Hades' from *Ulysses*.

I've chosen these texts bearing in mind the second and third of the aims listed above. Joyce is very much the *deliberate artist*. He took ten years to complete *The Portrait*, seven to write *Ulysses* and eighteen for *Finnegans Wake*. He's a kind of Milton of the Novel, doing everything 'at a stretch', and only once. Each new work seems to belong to a different order of literature from its predecessor. Contrast such a career with those of untidy, prolific, uneven, geniuses like Dickens, or Balzac, or even George Eliot and Henry James. They all develop, of course, but progressively, and between their first and last novels, there's a recognizable resemblance. Joyce seemed to develop in great leaps. I doubt if anybody could have predicted *Ulysses* from the author of *Dubliners*, or *Finnegans Wake* even from the former.

So a variety of texts is necessary both to suggest the scale of Joyce's work, and the deep-seated experimentalism that drove him from one kind of writing to another. I'm afraid that it may make for rather fragmentary reading, but to have settled for one text—say, *The Portrait*—would not I think have brought out Joyce's individuality, nor the ways in which he breaks with the nineteenth-century tradition.

This Unit is divided up as follows:

1 Information about, questions for study, and comments on, the set reading.

2 Sections on some aspects of Joyce's writing, formally considered:

(a) Epiphanies
(b) Realism
(c) The Artist as Priest

3 Discussion of points of contact with, and difference from, Joyce and earlier novelists.

If you haven't already read the texts, please do so now before going any further with the Unit.

Author's Acknowledgement

I would like to thank Arnold Kettle and Nick Furbank for their helpful comments on the first draft.   G. M.

SECTION ONE

1.1 'Eveline'

J oyce began the *Dubliners* stories in the summer of 1904. Invited to contribute something to the *Irish Homestead*, he wrote 'The Sisters' (published in July), following it with 'Eveline' (published in September) and 'After the Races' (published in December). It was in October that Joyce left Dublin for what turned out to be the beginning of his long stay in Trieste. Ellman[1] suggests that the general mood of the stories is represented by 'The Holy Office', a poem Joyce wrote during those months attacking the reigning figures of the Irish Literary Movement (Yeats, Lady Gregory, George Russell) for sentimentality and feeble idealism:

> . . . That they may dream their dreamy dreams
> I carry off their filthy streams
> For I can do those things for them
> Through which I lost my diadem,
> Those things for which Grandmother Church
> Left me severely in the lurch.
> Thus I relieve their timid arses
> Perform my office of Katharsis. . . .
>
> Levin, p. 347

It's an interesting idea that Joyce's purgative realism should make *possible* the vague dreams of the Celtic Twilight. The poem shows Joyce defining himself not only over against the current literary milieu, but as *necessary to it*. How far it voices the tone and attitude of the actual stories is another matter.

1.2 In the discussion about aesthetics in Chapter 5 of *The Portrait of the Artist as a Young Man*, Stephen insists that the artist is 'impersonal', taking no sides about the issues raised in his stories, but letting them speak for themselves.

Warehouses, Ringsend
(Phyllis Thompson)

[1] Ellman, R., *James Joyce*, p. 171.

O'Connell Bridge, Dublin c 1895 (National Library of Ireland)

The artist, like the God of creation, remains within or behind or beyond or above his handiwork, invisible, refined out of existence, indifferent, paring his fingernails.

Levin, p. 221

This is a version of a general reaction in the later nineteenth century against the moral tendentiousness associated with the overt presence of the author in his own work. You'll perhaps remember that issue in connection with George Eliot. Henry James's main way of getting rid of the author was to work through the consciousness of particular characters, confining the reader's knowledge of the situation to that of the character. Another alternative, associated with the French novelist, Flaubert (1821–80), and increasingly influential in England, was that of the detached reporter, presenting situations and people with faithful realism, in a formal posture of no-comment. That, of course, left the author room for manoeuvre by selective 'angling' of the report to *imply* comment, or at least, an attitude. In any case, 'detachment' is not necessarily the opposite of offering a point of view. It can be a point of view of its own. In *Dubliners* Joyce's principal method is that of the detached reporter, subtly varied by the single-consciousness approach, especially in stories centred on one character. We need to look out for a constant shifting between external observation (with a greater or lesser degree of irony spicing the formal detachment) and dramatization of a character's consciousness.

1.3 Questions for Study

(a) In the second paragraph of 'Eveline', what voices do you hear—the reporting narrator's or Eveline's, or both? Read also the paragraph beginning 'The evening deepened in the avenue' (p. 376) for the same point.

(b) What method does Joyce use in the final episode to make Eveline's feelings clear? Does he report, or dramatize, or use some other method?

(c) What picture of Eveline's father does the story convey? (Notice what he says, as well as what Eveline says of him.)

(d) 'As she mused the pitiful vision of her mother's life laid its spell upon her—that life of commonplace sacrifices closing in final craziness' (p. 377). Whose voice is this?

(e) Does the story explain why Eveline can't leave Dublin?

(f) What attitude towards Eveline does it leave us with? Detached? Ironic? Sympathetic? Pitying? Indifferent?

1.4 Discussion

(a) The narrator-reporter speaks in sentences like: 'Few people passed. The man out of the last house passed on his way home; she heard his footsteps clacking along the concrete . . .' But with 'clacking' we begin to sense Eveline's actual experience, and this prepares for *her* voice with its childish lilt, perhaps even the evocation of her voice *as a child*. 'Then a man from Belfast bought the field and built houses on it—not like their little brown houses, but bright brick houses with shining roofs.' But notice also that she has an adult voice (see paragraph beginning 'She had consented to go away', p. 374) for her immediate problems, which contrasts with the voice she uses for the past.

(b) Eveline's feelings about finally leaving Dublin with Frank are conveyed in 'A bell clanged upon her heart . . . All the seas of the world tumbled about her heart . . . Amid the seas she sent a cry of anguish.' (p. 376) This is not the narrator-reporter, detached, observant; nor is it the voice of Eveline's consciousness—such metaphors would hardly occur to her. It is the narrator in a new role, using vivid poetic speech to penetrate her anguish of paralysing fear. But it is unobtrusive enough to *seem* like a report.

(c) What Eveline's father says adds subtle touches of conceit and pretentiousness to the main picture of a violent bully.

(d) This seems to me a voice you would not expect in this story, the commentator's. Eveline hardly would use such language. Only Joyce the conscious satirist of 'The Holy Office'. But it is the only case, I think.

(e) I don't believe so. It simply presents Eveline's failure as a fact about her and her situation. It is, perhaps, prepared for by the evident strength of the hold upon her of past memories and the familiar pattern of life. But it remains unexplained. The character's predicament is stated, rather than explored.

(f) I leave you to decide that for yourself. You need to remember both the vivid account of her fears, and the final image of the 'helpless animal' incapable of human response.

1.5 'The Dead'

The last to be written of the *Dubliners* stories, 'The Dead' partly reflects a change in Joyce's attitude towards his native country. In September 1906, when he was working as bank clerk in Rome, he wrote to his brother:

Sometimes thinking of Ireland it seems to me that I have been unnecessarily harsh. I have reproduced (in *Dubliners* at least) none of the attraction of the city. . . . I have not reproduced its ingenuous insularity and its hospitality. The latter 'virtue' so far as I can see does not exist elsewhere in Europe.

Letters II, 166

Written during 1907, 'The Dead' makes Irish hospitality one of its themes, and more generally, replaces the satirical-pitying detachment of many stories with a more involved and sympathetic approach. Ellman suggests that it is Joyce's first 'song of exile' (p. 263). It is also on a bigger scale than the rest of the collection, and more complex in method. It was first published when *Dubliners* appeared as a whole in June 1914.

1.6 Questions for Study

I've arranged these questions so that they lead from points of detail to general interpretation.

(a) Read the first paragraphs on pp. 477 and 480. Whose voice speaks? The reporter-narrator, or one or other of the characters, or both?

(b) What is the effect when Molly Ivors leaves the party (p. 492)?

(c) In its presentation of the characters, does 'The Dead' use the same method as 'Eveline'?

(d) Snow is mentioned several times during the story. Look up the instances (pp. 478, 490, 497, 506, 514). What is the effect? Does snow 'symbolize' something, and if so, what?

(e) What impression of the Irish virtue of hospitality is conveyed by the party scenes?

(f) In the final episode, Gabriel and Gretta speak in distinct idioms. What do you make of this? What does it contribute to the impact of Gretta's story about Michael Furey?

(g) 'He saw himself as a ludicrous figure . . . the pitiable fatuous fellow he had caught a glimpse of in the mirror' (p. 511). Does the story confirm Gabriel's opinion of himself?

(h) 'One by one, they were all becoming shades. Better pass boldly into that other world, in the full glory of some passion, than fade and wither dismally with age' (p. 514). Is that the story's major point?

(i) Structurally, 'The Dead' seems to have two distinct parts: the dance at the Misses Morkan, which culminates in the applause following Gabriel's speech (pp. 477–500), and Gabriel's discovery of the true state of his marriage and his own nature (pp. 500–14). Does Joyce successfully connect the two parts? Is the first section too long? Is this a case of two rather different kinds of story, only loosely connected by Gabriel's role in each?

(j) What changes occur in Gabriel in the closing moments of the story?

(k) Who *are* 'the dead'?

(l) What do you notice about the prose style of the last paragraph?

1.7 Discussion

(a) I would think that Lily's is the main voice in the opening paragraph on p. 477. The narrator wouldn't use phrases like 'literally run off her feet', or 'it was well for her . . . ' The effect is to create a certain distance between us and the bustle of the arrivals. The paragraph on p. 480 begins with the

reporting narrator, but merges into Gabriel's voice. Clearly 'his whole speech was a mistake from first to last, an utter failure' reflects his mood, since the speech hasn't been delivered yet!

(b) It depresses Mary Jane, and Gabriel thinks it an example of the new generation's un-Irish rudeness. Do we share these feelings? Not altogether. Molly is lively, direct, and though critical of Gabriel, not unfriendly. I think there's a suggestion that she leaves because she's had enough of the annual ritual. Notice also the contrast between her spirited openness and Gabriel's role-playing.

(c) The minor characters are presented much in the manner of 'Eveline', externally, by report, with occasional transitions into the voice of a single character. But Gabriel is presented quite differently. We have direct access to his feelings, which we in part share. They are not simply observed and reported. Gabriel is one of the few characters in *Dubliners* who's explored in this 'inner' way. This is largely responsible for the different feeling about the Dubliners that emerges from this story.

(d) I'd prefer to call it a recurrent 'motif', rather than a 'symbol', because it has no fixed meaning. The recurrence creates what Forster in *Aspects of the Novel* calls a *rhythmic* effect, a way of unifying fictions more subtle than that of plot. At first, it suggests freedom, fresh air, an escape from the tensions of the party, which helps to convey Gabriel's underlying discomfort about his role, and perhaps even suggests something claustrophobic about the whole occasion. Later, though, it's reduced to the simpler role of being part of the weather, and finally in the last paragraph it's connected with Gabriel's mysterious final 'thoughts'. Here, possibly, it is reasonable to talk of 'symbol', though quite what it symbolises is not easy to say. See (j).

(e) Despite Joyce's intention of celebrating the Irish virtue of hospitality, the effect seems to me considerably more subtle. Gabriel's speech in praise of his aunts, and the applause and singing that follow, together perhaps with Freddy Malin's enthusiastic praise for Julia's singing, strike a genuine note. But a great deal of the occasion is registered through Gabriel's *anxiety* about it—his encounters with Lily, and Molly, and concern about his speech. Mary

10

Jane's musical performance is professional, rather than jolly, while the two most festive spirits, Mr Browne and Freddy Malins, are seen mainly as problems to be coped with, and Mr Browne's determined joking depresses everybody. The description of the supper table is attractive, but also extremely *formal*, and it's the arrangement of the food you remember—not the eating. Indeed, any spontaneous gaiety seems to be happening at the margins of the action. We get little sense of the physical activity needed for dancing lancers and quadrilles. The talk about singing is mainly about the past, and the people mainly in evidence are middle-aged, or old. (Molly Ivors, remember, leaves early.) So the reporting method *conceals* Joyce's selection, his slanting, of the whole account which seems to me to undermine any feeling of gaiety, warmth, hospitable fun. I don't mean that the good intentions of the Misses Morkan, or even Gabriel, are in any sense being criticized, but their result seems evanescent, insubstantial. See also (h), (i).

(f) Gabriel's speech usually involves adopting some style for the immediate occasion—to Lily in the opening scene, when he's eating his supper ('Kindly forget my existence . . . ladies and gentlemen'), when he asks the porter to take away the candle. He's inclined to pomposity, or at least, floweriness which reflects uneasiness about the kind of impression he'll make. There's equally a contrast between his real feelings and the way he behaves, which comes out in various oblique remarks. Thus, in the hotel with Gretta, he has to keep his actual feelings in check because of what he has learned about Michael Furey, so he tries irony. Her speech contrasts strikingly with all these complications. Its simple directness is of a piece with the tragic directness of her story. Joyce underlines this with one or two rural phrases: 'I used to go out walking with him', 'I was great with him at that time'. It's a brilliant contrast, I think, and crucial to the marvellously unrhetorical impact of 'I think he died for me'—which if it *weren't* unrhetorical, would leave an appalling impression. It's feeling at this level that undercuts Gabriel's world. He's incapable of it himself yet can recognize it as in some way fundamental. As readers, we gain a stronger impression of what Michael Furey was like from the way Gretta speaks, and still, to some extent, feels.

(g) The judgement clearly reflects Gabriel's mood at that point. So it's not the whole truth about him. But there's enough in it to substantiate the critical impression his behaviour at the party builds up—his self-concern, his reaction to Molly Ivors. It's an important retrospective comment, helping to link the two sections of the story, since the way Gabriel appears at the party is the necessary basis for the different Gabriel of the hotel scene.

(h) Another, even more important retrospective comment, linking the two sections. The quality of experience represented in Gretta's story about Michael Furey is held over against the pattern of life represented by the annual dance. Whether it is the *point* of the story, I leave you to decide.

(i) Perhaps only an extensive analysis of the story would really answer this question. The main connecting link is of course Gabriel. In the first section, Joyce builds up a number of impressions of him that provide the essential basis for his self-discovery in the second. Other links have been suggested in (d), (g) and (h). Perhaps the most explicit is Gabriel's thought on p. 513 that his aunt Julia will soon be dead, summing up the fragile quality in the hospitable bustle of the Misses Morkan. Generally, too, the contrast between the sections, both in method and substance, is deliberate. Where the first is social, public and externally reported, the second is private, intimate, impassioned and 'inner' in method. The story's movement is towards the mysterious depths of the last paragraph.

(j) I think the main points to notice are these: a new self-acceptance replacing the uneasy assertion of superiority characteristic of his earlier behaviour; a more truthful view of his wife replacing the romantic-aesthetic image conjured up when he sees her listening to the song (pp. 503–4); a more generous quality of feeling about others centred on the knowledge that everybody dies. There is also the strange experience of the last two paragraphs, where his 'soul approached the region where dwell the vast hosts of the dead'. Here is one critic's comment.

Reason and love, an unspectacular but visibly 'unresentful' and 'generous' love, replace [his earlier feelings] . . . And only now is Gabriel free, able to feel what the whole story has enacted: the complex tangle of distance and presence, passion and decay, love and detachment, aspiration and limit, life and death, in every individual and every society. The snow no longer represents to him the purity of the withdrawn self; as he 'swoons' into unconsciousness, it seems to fall 'like the descent of their last end, upon all the living and the dead'.[1]

Gabriel is falling asleep, but does that explain the puzzling sentence 'The time had come for him to set out on his journey westwards.'? Traditionally, the journey to the west suggests death, but we're hardly to suppose that Gabriel is dying. Has he then decided to take his wife to the Aran Isles, as Molly Ivors suggested, and Gretta would like? Yet what follows is an imaginary journey to Michael's Galway grave.

(k) Perhaps the question to ask is 'who are the living'? Michael Furey though dead, persists in Gretta's mind as an image of more intense life than anything else in the story. His influence demolishes Gabriel's living desire—such as it is. The life of the dance is, I've suggested, oddly insubstantial, impermanent. 'The dead' might be held to apply to the people who are prominent in it, or to their memories of the past. Yet the last paragraph points to a fundamental link between living and dead. So the title seems to apply both to different groups within the story for opposed reasons, and then to everybody for yet another. Ellman (pp. 258–9) makes the interesting suggestion that Gabriel suffers a kind of metaphorical death in the last paragraph, giving up his 'European' ideals of intellect and culture for 'Irish' direct passionate experience, a death of one kind of identity into the life of another, of the feelings and instincts. The story's title, at any rate, seems deliberately ambiguous.

(l) The striking feature of the last paragraph is, surely, the marked rhythm set up by the repetitions of 'falling', by the two inversions ('falling softly . . . softly falling', 'falling faintly ... faintly falling'), and by the pattern of sentences which follow the snow westward from Gabriel's window in Dublin towards the Galway gravestone. I've called this an aspect of 'style', but of course, it's what establishes the final mood. Just as Gabriel achieves a new insight into his own nature, he begins to share in the common experience of humanity through a recognition of death. (That seems to be why his 'soul swooned': he surrenders his carefully guarded individual identity.) The rhythm of the paragraph moves away from Gabriel towards a world beyond him—Michael Furey's passion and death, the Ireland outside of Dublin, the impersonal world of snow and night and river.

[1] Goldberg, S. L. in Garrett, Peter K. (ed.), *Twentieth Century Interpretations of 'Dubliners'*, Prentice-Hall, 1968, p. 92.

In January 1904, four months after his mother's death, Joyce wrote a narrative essay about his own character and development, and called it 'A Portrait of the Artist'. He submitted it for a new magazine called *Dana*. It was rejected partly for its obscurity. Challenged by this, Joyce decided to turn it into a novel. His brother noted in his diary:

Jim is beginning his novel, as he usually begins things, half in anger, to show that in writing about himself he has a subject of more interest than their (i.e. literary contemporaries) aimless discussion. . . . It is to be almost autobiographical, and naturally as it comes from Jim, satirical. He is putting a large number of his acquaintances into it, and those Jesuits whom he has known. I don't think they will like themselves in it.

Ellman, p. 153

The satirical title 'Stephen Hero' was decided on, and by the summer of 1904, Joyce had completed a sizeable volume. Most of the early chapters were lost, according to one report because Joyce threw the manuscript into the fire after repeated rejections. Some later chapters survived, however, and were published in 1944, edited by Theodore Spencer, as *Stephen Hero*.

In September 1907, shortly after completing 'The Dead', Joyce decided to rewrite *Stephen Hero* on an entirely new plan, condensing it into five long chapters. In the next six months he completed the first three, but the whole work was not finished till early in 1914, when Joyce sent it to Ezra Pound, who arranged to have it published in an *avant-garde* journal called *The Egoist*. There it appeared in instalments during 1915. It was first published in book form in 1917, dated 'Dublin 1904, Trieste 1914'.

Here is Pound's reaction to getting the last instalment:

I think the book is permanent like Flaubert and Stendahl. Not so squarish as Stendahl, certainly not so varnished as Flaubert. In english [sic] I think you join on to Hardy and Henry James (I don't mean a resemblance, I mean that there's been nothing of permanent value in prose in between) . . .

Hang it all, we don't get prose books that a man can *re*read. We don't get prose that gives us pleasure paragraph by paragraph.

Joyce also submitted the manuscript to a publisher called Duckworth, and it was reported on by Edward Garnett (a supporter of Conrad and of the young D. H. Lawrence). He wrote:

It is all ably written and the picture is curious. But the style is too discursive and his point of view will be called 'a little sordid'. It isn't a book that would make a young man's reputation—it is too unconventional for our British public. And in War Time it has less chance than at any other.

Decline with thanks.[1]

1.9   The substantial difference between the original *Stephen Hero* and the final *Portrait* lies in the latter's concentration on a single theme—the hero's development *as an artist*. Everything else in the novel—his family and friends, his religion, his education, his country's politics—exists in relation to that theme. The result is a packed, condensed, sharply focused work, with scarcely a detail that doesn't bear pondering. But there is also a significant change of method. In *Stephen Hero* the author's attitude towards Stephen is explicit: part satirical

---

[1] Anderson, Chester G. (ed.), *James Joyce: A Portrait of the Artist as a Young Man*, Viking Press, 1968, pp. 317, 319.

as the original choice of title implied, and part admiring. But in the *Portrait* the author has become as 'invisible' as Stephen's aesthetic theory requires. The story is primarily told through Stephen's consciousness. In *Dubliners* we saw that the external, observing point of view was occasionally varied by transitions in and out of the consciousness of the single character. In the *Portrait* the emphasis has been reversed. Joyce uses the reporter's stance to give Stephen's experience objectivity. There is no 'I' telling the story, no formal admission of Stephen's subjectivity in relation to a world outside him. Yet everything is experienced by Stephen, and in relation to him, and only his thoughts and feelings matter. This leads to some uncertainty about how Stephen's opinions and judgements are to be judged by the reader. In a novel about growing up, the hero will make mistakes, reveal immaturities. But in the *Portrait*, Joyce allows the reader no explicit point of view other than Stephen's, so exactly when he is to be agreed with, and when observed and judged is not always clear. It's not, I think, a difficulty for our limited purposes, but if you get the chance to read the whole work at a later stage, bear it in mind. If you are not quite sure what to think of Stephen, you will find yourself in distinguished critical company.

Unlike the two *Dubliners* stories, Chapter One of the *Portrait* is not a self-contained work, so our discussion of it must be inevitably limited, and even a bit artificial. But I think we can at least find out *how* the whole novel needs to be read, and what is new about Joyce's methods.

1.10   Questions for Study (1)

First, some general impressions.

(a) You've read other novels in this course partly, or wholly, centred on a child's experience. What, if anything, is new about Joyce's handling of the issue?

(b) What do you notice about the narrative structure?

(c) You've met the term 'stream of consciousness' in Unit 30 (p. 9). Does Joyce use the technique here?

(d) How does Joyce convey the subjective intensity of Stephen's experiences?

(e) Can you describe in one adjective what strikes you as *individual* about Joyce's work?

1.11   **Discussion**

(a) Surely Joyce is far more thorough-going than any previous novelist about keeping close to the way a young child experiences the world. Stephen thinks and speaks like a small boy, not a disguised adult. (Contrast Maisie. And even Pip? Huck Finn provides the nearest approach, but he's older, and more reflective.) Joyce's fidelity to the actual—in the first instance, his own memories—is in one respect revolutionary. *The contents of Stephen's mind are rarely thoughts, but feeling and perceptions*. The first page and a half is the most striking case. Stephen's earliest memories are those of a very young child exploring the world through direct physical sensation, closely associated with his relations with father and mother. In other words, here is a fictional version of the kind of thing modern psychology has only since established about the basis of an infant's experience.

(b) Overt narrative has been largely dropped. The story cuts from episode to episode in cinematic fashion, and from present, to past, to future time, without forewarning. The reader is left to work out for himself the connections between Stephen's four vividly remembered episodes of home and school life. The Christmas dinner scene, for example, hardly involves him, except as a witness. Dante says:

—O, he'll remember all this when he grows up . . . the language he heard against God and religion and priests in his own home.

—Let him remember too, cried Mr Casey to her from across the table, the language with which the priests and the priests' pawns broke Parnell's heart and hounded him into his grave. Let him remember that too when he grows up.

Levin, pp. 74–5

We already know that Stephen is remembering it in the most compelling detail. Here it is presented without comment. Only later in the novel do we find out how it affected him. Joyce expects the reader to recognize, without further information, that the scene is powerfully influential on his hero's development. If you contrast that with Dickens's explicit placing of clues for the reader early in Pip's life, you'll see how much more Joyce wants us to do.

The original text, incidentally, asterisks the transitions between the episodes. The asterisks have been dropped from the Penguin text, but the divisions are still abrupt enough to be noticeable (pp. 53, 69, 79).

(c) Any sustained attempt to work through a single consciousness begins to overlap with 'stream of consciousness' methods: in the first Clongowes episode, say, the interplay of actual experience with nostalgic memory and future longing, or the blurring of the line between reality and dream in the infirmary scene. But I think it would be a mistake to use the description here. Joyce's reporting third-person technique maintains a certain objectivity, a reference to a world not wholly dependent on Stephen's consciousness. It's perhaps a half-way stage between the largely external emphasis of *Dubliners*, and the method of *Ulysses* (para. 1.17).

(d) Mainly by concentrating on his physical *sensations*, for instance, when he's ill, or when he is pandied rather than on any account of his *feelings*.

(e) An unfair question! But I hope you tried it. My choice would be 'disciplined'.

1.12   Questions for Study (2)

Some more detailed points to consider:

(a) How far does Stephen's speech style in the first, third and fourth episodes, reflect his increasing age? Choose typical passages from each.

(b) In the first episode, are Stephen's memories at random or do they follow a pattern (other than chronological)?

(c) Re-read the opening paragraphs of the second episode (as far as 'from seventyseven to seventysix' (p. 55)). Make notes on the interplay of the narrator's voice and Stephen's.

(d) How does the theme of the *artist* appear in the chapter?

(e) Association of ideas (or memories, or feelings) is more typical of the working of human consciousness, than logical connection. Has Joyce made use of this fact?

(f) Both Clongowes episodes involve reference to the 'square'—the outside lavatories used by the boys. Is this accidental?

(g) What is your attitude to Stephen's dream-death thoughts about Wells, and magnanimity about Fr Dolan? (pp. 64–5, 95).

(h) Stephen is fairly passive in this chapter. Do you see any connection between this impression and Joyce's method? Do you see any resemblance between him and the main characters in the two *Dubliners* stories?

1.13   **Discussion**

(a) Stephen's speech alters as he grows up. In the first episode his sentences are very simple. 'He sang that song. That was his song . . . When you wet the bed first it is warm then it gets cold. His mother put on the oilsheet. That had the queer smell.' (p. 53) In the second episode, a new boy at school, his speech echoes that of the other boys: 'Rody Kickham was a decent fellow but Nasty Roche was a stink.' (p. 54) But he also has his own voice:

What did that mean, to kiss? You put your face up like that to say good night and then his mother put her face down. That was to kiss. His mother put her lips on his cheek; her lips were soft and they wetted his cheek; and they made a tiny little noise: kiss. Why did people do that with their two faces?

p.59

Here is Stephen's inquiring speculative mind, examining experience and language. And again in the third episode there is a different quality.

It was easy what he had to do. All he had to do was when the dinner was over and he came out in his turn to go on walking but not out to the corridor but up the staircase on the right that led to the castle. He had nothing to do but that; to turn to the right and walk fast up the staircase and in half a minute he would be in the low dark corridor that led through the castle to the rector's room.   p.91

The sentences are governed not by a thought-out structure, but—boy-like— by the succession of concrete experiences he is imagining, as well as by the rhythm of his determination to go through with it. These language differences are an index of Joyce's way of registering a child's experience.

(b) Stephen's memories seem random at first, but I think they reflect a pattern. His father is at the centre of the first group; then there is his song; then his mother dominates the second, which ends in his dance; then other adults are brought in, ending in the poem. One critic has suggested a grouping based on the senses: sound (the story about the moo cow), sight (his father's beard), taste (lemon platt), touch (wetting the bed), smell (the oilcloth, his mother).

(c) The first paragraph of the second episode opens with the narrator describing the playgrounds at Clongowes; then telling us what Stephen is *doing*; then what he is *feeling*; and finally, in the last two sentences, Stephen's voice takes over, and continues through the next paragraph. In the reported conversation that follows, Joyce uses the pluperfect tense 'had asked . . . had answered . . . had said'. This could be either the narrator telling us directly what *had* happened, or what Stephen *remembered* as having happened. It balances between report, and dramatization. The next paragraph has this:

He crept about from point to point on the fringe of his line, making little runs now and then. But his hands were bluish with cold. He kept his hands in the side pockets of his belted grey suit. That was a belt round his pocket. And belt was also to give a fellow a belt.

p. 54

The narrator again tells us what Stephen is doing and feeling, then is suddenly replaced by Stephen's voice reflecting on the two meanings of 'belt'. I think these transitions ultimately blur the distinction between the narrator and Stephen, as if he were both narrator *and* protagonist, sometimes telling his own story in a very detached way, at others dramatizing it.

In the next paragraph, Stephen's voice reports his own memories, using the pluperfect tense, i.e. he narrates his own past. The final paragraph begins with the narrator and finishes with Stephen.

Mainly then, we hear Stephen's voice, and the narrator's function seems to be to give distance and objectivity to his experience. We move away from Stephen but only momentarily. There is no narrating personality, alternative to Stephen, offering another view of his situation or even sustaining a neutral detachment. The two voices interplay continuously.

(d) Mainly, through Stephen's interest in language and words. Notice this pattern: his rhyme 'Apologize', the sentences from the spelling book that resemble poetry; his imaginative response to the rituals of his religion; and his interest in the symbolism of terms like Tower of Ivory and House of Gold.

(e) Joyce uses association deliberately, but also unobtrusively:

How cold and slimy the water had been! A fellow had once seen a big rat jump into the scum. Mother was sitting at the fire with Dante waiting for Brigid to bring in the tea. She had her feet on the fender and her jewelly slippers were so hot and they had such a lovely warm smell!

p. 55

The shift from his present condition (fevered), the cause (being knocked into the scummy water), to the security of home needs no comment. But notice that his mother is originally connected with putting on the oilsheet after he'd wet the bed. 'That had the queer smell . . . His mother had a nicer smell than his father.' (p. 53) The pattern of water/mother/smell underlies the connection here. Most of Stephen's thinking in the second episode is controlled by associations like this. That's why it's not altogether mistaken to remember the 'stream of consciousness' method.

(f) In the second episode Stephen is knocked into the scummy 'square ditch' behind the lavatories; in the fourth, the 'square' is connected with the homosexual offences and so with the flogging of the offenders; while in the first episode, Stephen wets his bed. Natural functions are intensely important to children, partly as physical sensations, partly because they're half-taboo, and

George Clancy, J. F. Byrne and Joyce while at University College, Dublin (Croessman Collection of James Joyce, Southern Illinois University at Carbondale)

learning to control them is so important to the all-powerful adults. I don't think there's any 'meaning' to be taken from this pattern. Stephen's curiosity about the 'smugging' in the lavatories can be explained on grounds of accurate observation. but the pattern doesn't seem accidental. (Notice also that Stephen's one interpolation in the second episode is his comment on Mr Casey spitting in the old woman's eye—not *nice*, thinks Stephen.)

(g) I'd suggest these are examples where we can't be sure what Joyce wants us to feel. Are we being presented with a neutral report, or are we meant to notice Stephen's self-dramatization? In the final episode, Stephen doesn't really join in the celebration: he's the object of it, then goes off on his own and has forgiving thoughts about Fr Dolan. Is there irony here, or not? It seems to me left open. This problem is more pervasive later in the novel. Notice that it doesn't exist in the third episode. None of the parties to the quarrel invites special sympathy, though in the end, the Parnell side is more attractive because of the different quality of feeling it calls up in its defenders.

(h) Stephen is passive. But he does one thing—confronts the Rector on a point of principle. This combination of unassertive outward behaviour and intense, and independent, moral and intellectual life is not only a major trait of Stephen, but so intimately connected with Joyce's *method*, that you might almost argue the latter grew out of his conception of Stephen.

In the outward world, Stephen merely exists, and is acted on. The narrator reports all this, flatly, neutrally. But when experience is reflected on or examined Stephen's voice takes over. Hence the mixture of narrator and dramatization we noticed in (c). The outward world is there mainly for Stephen to react to—intellectually, aesthetically—to digest its meaning. There does also seem to be a connection between the passivity of Eveline and Stephen, and even of Gabriel, who is uncomfortable in the world of action, at his most individual when thinking and observing. I think that we begin to grasp Joyce's vision of experience in this sort of connection.

1.14   *Ulysses*

Joyce got the idea for *Ulysses* in 1907 when he planned a *Dubliners* story of that title, about a Dublin Jew rumoured to be a cuckold. But he made no progress with it till 1914, when he was finishing *The Portrait*. By that date his conception of fiction had greatly changed, and the novel, growing progressively more complex, took up all his creative energy over the next seven years. He began it in Trieste, before the outbreak of the 1914-18 war. In 1915, because of the war, he moved with his family to Zürich, a lively, cosmopolitan city in neutral Switzerland (where also resided the psycho-analyst C. G. Jung, and during the war years, Lenin). Much of *Ulysses* was written in Zürich, and in 1918 Joyce became friendly with a British artist, Frank Budgen, talking extensively with him about the scope and structure of the work.

'I am writing a book,' said Joyce, 'based on the wanderings of Ulysses. The *Odyssey*, that is to say, serves me as a ground plan. Only my time is recent time and all my hero's wanderings take no more than eighteen hours.'

Budgen, p. 15

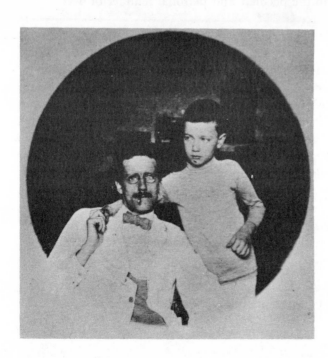

*James Joyce and son—
photographed during their
period in Trieste (Croessman
Collection of James Joyce,
Southern Illinois University
at Carbondale)*

Joyce's hero is a Dublin Jew, called Leopold Bloom, a small-time canvasser for advertisements. The novel covers one day in his life, 16 June 1904. The two other main characters are Stephen Dedalus, a little older than the hero of *The Portrait*, and seen in more critical light; and Bloom's wife Molly, who in the course of the novel entertains (off-stage) her lover, Blazes Boylan. Bloom knows about the rendezvous, and during his wanderings round Dublin, it is never far from his mind. During the day Bloom and Stephen pass each other once or twice and when they finally meet, establish an implicit father-son relationship.

But this account of the 'story' is almost marginal to the impact of the book, which is unlike any other previous novel. Three points may be mentioned here. In presenting Bloom, Stephen and Molly, Joyce used a device called 'monologue intérieur',[1] which he said he took from a minor French novelist, but which, as Ellman has pointed out (p. 368), can also be seen as a development from *The Portrait*, with its concentration on a single consciousness. The intention in *Ulysses* is to give the reader a more than usually thorough knowledge of the character by sharing in all his thoughts however private, or half-suppressed. The implication of the method is that reality exists in the individual consciousness of the world and Joyce was not the only novelist to think so. (See Unit 29 on D. H. Lawrence.) Another name for this technique is, of course, 'stream of consciousness'. If you want to find out how Stephen and Molly appear in the novel, dip into the sections in Levin's text called 'Nestor' and 'Penelope'. Bloom is well represented in the set reading, 'Hades'.

A second point is the immensely detailed account of these lives, and the bewildering accumulation of other detail in the form of minor characters, places, memories, events, all connected in some way with Bloom's ordinary experience in Dublin on 16 June 1904. You can get a glimpse of that in the section called 'The Wandering Rocks'. Budgen remarks of Joyce's interest in detail:

In the course of many walks with Joyce in Zürich I found that for him human character was best displayed . . . in the commonest acts of life. How a man ties his shoe-laces or how he eats his egg will give a better clue to his differentiation than how he goes forth to war. . . . Character, in short, lay not in the doing or not doing of a grand action, but in the peculiar and personal manner of performing a simple one.

Budgen, p. 75

The third point is the dazzling variety of styles deployed by Joyce throughout the novel to reflect different episodes, different times of day, different subordinate themes. The section called 'Sirens' for example, attempts to reflect a musical style in its prose rhythms, its fragments of song, its operatic manner as a whole. This emphasis on 'style' grew as the novel progressed. One section narrates its episode by an imitation of the different English prose styles since Anglo-Saxon times to Joyce's own day. Another imitates the style of day-dream romantic stories for contemporary women's magazines. These different styles are not always expressive, but certainly in the earlier part of the novel, Joyce shows an astounding ability, sensitively to vary the style within the limits set by the relevant character. Elsewhere, however, the reader is sometimes wearied by the endless rhetorical *tour de force*.

Ulysses began to appear in *The Little Review* in March 1918. When the war ended, Joyce took his family back to Trieste, but finding it too much changed,

---

[1] H. Sykes Davies referred to it in Radio 15.

moved to Paris in 1920, where *Ulysses* was finally completed. The last instalment, 'Penelope', was published in October 1921. The book version was printed in Paris, early in 1922, it being impossible to find English printers. For many years, it was banned from Ireland, England, and America. But its publication put Joyce at the head of the avant-garde movement in post-war fiction, and from that date, his years of relative obscurity were over. T. S. Eliot wrote one of the most intelligent of the early appreciations, claiming that Joyce's use of a myth as the organizing principle of his work had 'the importance of a scientific discovery'.[1] Its impact on an Irish writer of an elder generation may be judged by this:

Dear Madam,

I have read several fragments of *Ulysses* in its serial form. It is a revolting record of a disgusting phase of civilisation; but it is a truthful one . . . to me it is all hideously real. I have walked those streets and known those shops and have heard and taken part in those conversations. I escaped from them to England at the age of twenty; and forty years later have learnt from the books of Mr. Joyce that Dublin is still what it was. . . .

I must add, as the prospectus implies an invitation to purchase, that I am an elderly Irish gentleman, and that if you imagine that any Irishman, much less an elderly one, would pay 150 francs for a book, you know little of my countrymen.

Faithfully,

G. Bernard Shaw

Letters, I. 50

1.15 There are no chapter breaks in *Ulysses*, but instead eighteen sections distinguished from each other in a number of ways—by the hour of the day, by the style, by a dominant colour in the imagery and description, by a dominant organ of the human body (heart, lungs, brain, and so forth). Each section is also based on an episode in Homer's poem and Joyce entitled them accordingly —'Nestor', 'Circe', 'Penelope'—though only in discussing the novel with his friends. No titles appear in the text. The 'Hades' section is based on Odysseus' visit to the underworld, where he converses with the spirits of dead companions and learns his ultimate fate—years of wandering before his return home. In Joyce's novel, Bloom journeys with some Dublin acquaintances to Glasnevin Cemetery for the funeral of Paddy Dignam. The Penguin selection prints the second half of Joyce's text, beginning with the arrival at the Cemetery, omitting Bloom's journey through the Dublin streets, where he shares a funeral carriage with Martin Cunningham, Simon Dedalus, and Mr Power. None the less, though only a fragment of the novel, the extract fairly represents Joyce's general method in *Ulysses*, and gives a reliable impression of its hero, Leopold Bloom.

1.16 Questions for Study

Read the extract now, and make a few notes on these points:

(a) How do we recognize the difference between Bloom's voice, and that of the narrator?

(b) What is the effect of the alternation of Bloom's and the narrator's voice?

(c) Are Bloom's thoughts at random, or do you notice a pattern of any kind?

(d) What sort of person is Bloom?

[1] Robert H. Leming, *James Joyce: The Critical Heritage*, 1970, I, 270.

(e) Has the episode a theme, or any overriding 'point'?

Discussion

(a) Bloom and the narrator have distinct language styles. Here is the narrator:

A team of horses passed from Finglas with a toiling plodding tread, dragging through the funereal silence a creaking waggon on which lay a granite block. The waggoner marching at their head saluted.

Levin, p. 28

Using normal English sentences of a noun-verb-object structure, the narrator describes and reports scenes and actions, on the whole neutrally. Bloom's voice follows immediately after:

Coffin now. Got here before us, dead as he is. Horse looking round at it with his plume skeowways. Dull eye: collar tight on his neck pressing a bloodvessel or something.

Instead of whole sentences, Bloom tends to use phrases, nouns without articles, missed out predicates. That is the grammatical way to put it. What is the different effect? We are observing the same scene, but more particularly, with a stronger sense of participating in its physical reality. The narrator sees 'a team of horses', reports sounds, as from a distance. Bloom notices one horse, its funeral plume awry, its eye, and horse collar, and its particular movements. His style is packed, elliptical, and reflects not just what he sees, but what he thinks. He goes on:

Do they (i.e. the horses) know what they cart out here every day? Must be twenty or thirty funerals every day. Then Mount Jerome for the protestants. Funerals all over the world everywhere every minute. Shovelling them under by the cartload doublequick. Thousands every hour. Too many in the world.

(Mount Jerome was a cemetery for Protestants.)

Bloom has an imaginative, speculative mind. He wonders why the horse has turned his head, then whether it knows what it is doing. That leads him by a natural, but omitted, link of association to the daily number of funerals at Glasnevin alone. Then from Catholic to Protestant burials, and so to the number going on in the world every minute. In a sentence like 'shovelling them under by cartload doublequick', his practical, unsentimental attitude to burial (already implicit in the opening remarks), surfaces. You can't, in fact, say much about Bloom's language without taking up the question of his character. Perhaps you've noticed that already in your notes on (d), but if not, then before going further, choose some sentences or a paragraph that seems to you to express his main traits.

(b) The immediate effect of the contrast between Bloom and the narrator is to keep the reader on his toes.

The mutes shouldered the coffin and bore it through the gates. So much dead weight. Felt heavier myself stepping out of the bath. First the stiff: then the friends of the stiff. Corny Kelleher and the boy followed with their wreaths. Who is that beside them? Ah, the brother-in-law.

p. 28

Joyce doesn't let the reader settle down either with the narrator's or Bloom's tone. We shift from observation of the scene, to Bloom's imaginative participation in it, to his sardonic comment, back to observation, and finally to another of Bloom's traits, his quick interest in people. Such contrasts sharpen our sense of Bloom's difference from the world described by the narrator. They underline his highly individual mind, probing and reflecting on his immediate experience.

There's also an effect that seems to me 'structural': the rhythm set up by the alteration of the objective narrator, and Bloom's subjective reactions, which is almost more prominent than the faint narrative thread (the progress of the funeral) holding the episode together. 'Story' here, in the usual sense, is at a minimum. What I remember of 'Hades' is the rhythmic interchange between Bloom's mind and the rest of the world.

Notice also that Joyce gives the narrator more than one role. Consider this example:

The coffin dived out of sight, eased down by the men straddled on the grave-trestles. They struggled up and out: and all uncovered. Twenty.

Pause.

If we were all suddenly somebody else.

Far away a donkey brayed. Rain. No such ass. Never see a dead one, they say. Shame of death. They hide. Also poor papa went away.

Gentle sweet air blew round the bared heads in a whisper. Whisper. The boy by the graveyard held his wreath with both hands staring quietly in the black open space. Mr Bloom moved behind the portly kindly caretaker. Well cut frockcoat. Weighing them up perhaps to see which will go next. . . .

p. 37

Mainly, the narrator presenting the scene alternates with Bloom's thoughts about it. But in two cases, the narrator's idiom is unexpected. If you haven't noticed this, re-read the passage.

The two expressions sound at first unlike the narrator, because they consist of single words seeming to represent longer sentences or phrases. The first is 'pause'. Is this an abbreviated version of 'There was a pause'? Perhaps, but the effect is of an imperative, a request to the reader to take part in the experience, so that the next phrase ('If we are all suddenly somebody else') which is Bloom's thought, seems to include *us*. The second case is 'whisper', where the narrator directly conveys both the effect of the air he has just described, and the sounds of the mourners whispering. In both instances the narrator seems more like the producer of a play, than a reporter. He conveys experiences, as well as describes them. So the relation between Bloom and the narrator is here more complex. Instead of contrasting with the other mourners, Bloom's feelings about his father's death make individual and specific what they are all feeling. The narrator's sentence about the air blowing on the bared heads holds the experience of shared grief, concentrates it in the image of the boy looking into the open grave, then the feeling moves off into Bloom's sardonic thought about the caretaker. It's an extraordinary moment, I think, subtly and deeply felt, expressed in brilliantly original and sensitive art. I'll come back to the method in Section 2.

23

(c) Bloom's thoughts may often have seemed to you random. Things come into his mind: his father's death, his son's ('poor little Ruddy'), his wife Molly, individuals like Mrs Sinico, Alderman Hooper—about whom we know, at this point, little—and for no apparent reason. But probably you noticed distinct patterns, or rhythms, in his thinking. Depth, naturally is his main topic, and every now and again, sex. He has flights of fancy of a curiously practical kind. His shrewd, critical, sardonic comments combine with a steadily compassionate feeling for other men: his thoughts about Dignam's son, or the well-meaning caretaker, for example. And there is an underlying melancholy about the reality of death. Here is his reaction to part of the funeral service.

—*Et ne nos inducas in tentationem.*

The server piped the answers in the treble. I often thought it would be better to have boy servants. Up to fifteen or so. After that of course. . . .

Holy water that was, I expect. Shaking sleep out of it. He (i.e. the priest) must be fed up with that job, shaking that thing over all the corpses they trot up. What harm if he could see what he was shaking it over. Every mortal day: middleaged men, old women, children, women dead in childbirth, men with beards, baldheaded business men, consumptive girls with little sparrow's breasts. All the year round he prayed the same thing over them all and shook water on top of them: sleep. On Dignam now.

—*In paradisum.*

Said he was going to paradise or is in paradise. Says that over everybody. Tiresome kind of job. But he has to say something.

p. 31

Presumably the Latin phrase ('And lead us not into temptation') leads Bloom to his unexpected thought about boy servers being unsuitable beyond fifteen, when their voices break, and sex begins to 'tempt' them. Then there is his reductive commonsense about what the priest is doing ('shaking that thing over all the corpses they trot up'), and humane grasp of how boring it must be. Notice how his thoughts about the succession of corpses sustains nevertheless the idea of birth and life: children, childbirth, girls with immature breasts. His dismissive attitude towards funeral ceremonies is complemented by a compassionate response for the *fact* of death. And the rhythm of the prose changes in a remarkable way. (Read the paragraph aloud if you missed this.)

All the year round he prayed the same thing over them all and shook water on top of them: sleep. On Dignam now.

—*In paradisum.*

The water is no longer 'holy'. It just gives 'sleep'. The sardonic attitude changes to a deep tender feeling as the rhythm stops on 'sleep'—it is nearly a prayer—then rounds off with 'on Dignam now'. When the priest's Latin returns, it has a solemn ritual beauty independent of the religious meaning that Bloom's next comment ('But he has to say something') demolishes. An extract like this suggests that quite apart from the recurrence of certain topics in his mind, his thinking has a rhythm, a shape, reflecting a subtly individual interplay of attitudes. I think the point is worth insisting on a little, because while 'stream of consciousness', or 'interior monologue' are clearly helpful terms for describing Joyce's method here, they don't reflect the *shaping* element in Bloom's thought. It's not inappropriate to think of his more developed meditations as having something like 'poetic form', not because he is in any useful sense 'a poet', but rather because that is how Joyce conceived a mature and active mind.

(d) I've already conveyed a good deal of my impression of Bloom. Two points should be added. He's got an unconsciously funny side:

Besides how could you remember everybody? Eyes, walk, voice. Well, the voice, yes: gramophone. Have a gramophone in every grave or keep it in the house. After dinner on a Sunday. Put on old greatgrandfather Kraahraark! Hellohellohello amawfullyglad kraark awfullygladaseeragain hellohello amarawf kopthsth.

p. 40

Before hi-fi, I suppose one should add. Bloom seems to take his idea seriously.

He's also got a morbid side, it seems to me: his gothic speculations on sex in graveyards, and imaginative excitement about the activities of the rats, and the corpse-filled ground. I suppose the latter can be defended as humanistic realism. The body rots away, and there's nothing left to be resurrected. Yet there seems something over-intense about Bloom's interest. But having said that, it's crucial also to stress his energetic rejection of the grave.

The gates glimmered in front: still open. Back to the world again. Enough of this place. Brings you a bit nearer every time. ... I do not like that other world she wrote. No more do I. Plenty to see and hear and feel yet. Feel live warm beings near you. Let them sleep in their maggoty beds. They are not going to get me this innings. Warm beds: warm fullblooded life.

p. 41

Bloom's visit to 'Hades' reveals his moral independence, the key to the sense in which he is a genuine hero, a real modern Ulysses. He conquers death, not in the Christian way, but by facing it humanely, clear-sightedly, with comic practical schemes, with tender elegiac feeling, with a shrewd refusal to be taken in by funeral pomp. Perhaps this comes out more clearly if you compare it with Dickens's attitude towards funeral celebrations in *Great Expectations* (Ch. 35): satirical, wonderfully funny, but directed merely at false social attitudes, without any grappling with the actual experience of death and bereavement. Bloom gives, for what it is worth, and that's clearly a matter for debate, one possible answer: live while you can.

(e) The theme of the episode is, I imagine, clear enough: attitudes towards death. There is a polemical element that perhaps needs stressing: Bloom's secular humanism versus the Catholic Christian attitude, represented by the priest ('bully about the muzzle he looks. Bosses the show. Muscular Christian' (p. 30)), and by the other mourners. In the earlier part of 'Hades', Mr Power, expressing a conventional point of view, refers to suicide as the worst of actions. Bloom, in contrast, says that Dignam's death, being very sudden, is the best kind, a remark greeted by his companions with disapproving silence. In the cemetery, the other mourners seem at home, known to the caretaker, anxious to visit familiar graves of celebrated Irish patriots like O'Connell and Parnell. In this context, consider Bloom's thought about burial.

Poor Dignam! His last lie on the earth in his box. When you think of them all it does seem a waste of wood. All gnawed through. They could invent a handsome bier with a kind of panel sliding let it down that way. Ay but they might object to be buried out of another fellow's. They're so particular. Lay me in my native earth. Bit of clay from the holy land. Only a mother and deadborn child ever buried in the one coffin. I see what it means, I see. To protect him as long as possible even in the earth. *An Irishman's house is his coffin.*

pp. 36–7, my italics

Parnell's Grave, Glasnevin, Dublin 1891 (National Library of Ireland)

Joyce seems to aim deliberately here at something in Irish society. Bloom's resistance to the whole atmosphere of this Hades gets no support from his companions. If he is Ulysses, they are 'shades', dwellers in the underworld whose priest is Father Coffey, and whose idols symbolize a kind of Irish Nationalism that, in Joyce's eyes, distracted from the actual needs of contemporary Ireland. It is a subtler, less obtrusive, expression of the bitter debate about Parnell in *The Portrait of the Artist*.

1.18 In the next section I discuss some general points about Joyce's methods. Before going on to it, make some notes on your present impression of the difference between Joyce and novelists of the previous century. Here are some headings which may be helpful for crystallizing your thoughts.

(a) Story (or Plot)
(b) Characterization
(c) Structure
(d) Language

2.1 'Epiphanies'

Joyce is unusual among novelists for having developed definite ideas about his art at a very early stage of his career, when he'd written almost nothing of the work which made him famous. There's a reflection of this in the *Portrait*, where Stephen, still a student, expounds an elaborate aesthetic theory, and quotes in his support the medieval Christian theologian, St Thomas Aquinas (see Levin, p. 215ff.). Or again, in the *Portrait's* earlier version, *Stephen Hero*, he uses Aquinas to defend his essay on aesthetics against the threatened censorship of his college Principal. Both the theory itself, and the particular tactic used in its defence—rather as if D. H. Lawrence had appealed to Erasmus for support—are worth noticing. Novelists like Dickens and George Eliot assume a certain freedom for their art, and when they theorize about their own practice, they appeal to the authority of other *novelists*. Joyce's Roman

Trieste: Piazza Goldoni 1910 (Rod. Woitech, Trieste, Courtesy H. C. White Collection)

Trieste: Piazza Ponterosso 1910 (Leopold Rosenthal Druck Verlag, Trieste, Courtesy H. C. White Collection)

Fiume: Hotel Lloyd, Piazza Dante (Adamich) 1910 (Leopold Rosenthal Druck Verlag, Trieste, Courtesy H. C. White Collection)

Catholic education, and the cultural narrowness (he himself used more abusive terms) of Irish life seem to have forced him into an explicit defence of artistic freedom, using the most effective weapons for his purpose—an authority in his own Church.

2.2 Critics differ about the value of the aesthetic views put forward in the *Portrait*, especially in their relation to Joyce's own work. It can be argued that they're really Stephen's ideas, an index of his earnest immaturity, rather than Joyce's. But there's fairly general agreement that one notion, sketched out in *Stephen Hero*, though not in the *Portrait*, is central to an understanding of Joyce's art. Here is the relevant extract.

A young lady was standing on the steps of one of those brown brick houses which seem the very incarnation of Irish paralysis. A young gentleman was leaning on the rusty railings of the area. Stephen as he passed on his quest heard the following fragment of colloquy out of which he received an impression keen enough to afflict his sensitiveness very severely.

The Young Lady—(drawling discreetly) . . . O, yes . . . I was . . . at the . . . cha . . . pel . . .

The Young Gentleman—(inaudibly) . . . I . . . (again inaudibly) . . . I . . .

The Young Lady—(softly) . . . O . . . but you're . . . ve . . . ry . . . wick . . ed . . .

This triviality made him think of collecting many such moments in a book of epiphanies. By an epiphany he meant a sudden spiritual manifestation, whether in vulgarity of speech or of gesture or in a memorable phrase of the mind itself. He believed that it was for the man of letters to record these epiphanies with extreme care, seeing that they themselves are the most delicate and evanescent of moments.

Stephen Hero, p. 188

28

'Epiphany', a Greek word in origin, means 'a manifestation, a showing-forth'.
A friend of Joyce in his student days, Oliver St John Gogarty, recorded an
evening spent with Joyce and others, when the budding novelist said 'Excuse
me', and left the room. Gogarty goes on:

I don't mind being reported, but to be an unwilling contributor to one of his
Epiphanies is irritating.

Probably Fr Darlington had taught him, as an aside in his Latin class—for
Joyce knew no Greek—that 'Epiphany' meant 'a showing forth'. So he recorded under 'Epiphany' any showing forth of the mind by which he considered one gave oneself away.

Which of us had endowed him with an 'Epiphany' and sent him to the lavatory
to take it down?

As I Was Walking Down Sackville Street, p. 285

Somebody, however, brought up as a devout Catholic could hardly have failed
to know about the Feast of the Epiphany, which celebrated the showing of the
Infant Christ to the Magi. Joyce, in fact, seems to have adapted the term from
its devotional and theological context to his own literary-critical use.[1]

2.3   Gogarty, though, was right about Joyce's seriousness on the issue. Like Stephen
in *Stephen Hero*, Joyce did make a collection of 'epiphanies', and told his brother
that if he died 'copies of both his verses and epiphanies should be sent to all the
great libraries of the world, the Vatican not excepted' (Ellmann, p. 113).
The 'epiphanies' are short prose pieces—dialogue, descriptions, general reflections—sometimes autobiographical, dating mainly from the period 1901
to 1903, when in fact Joyce was still a student.[2] Joyce evidently thought of them
as self-subsistent records of moments of insight, meaningful in their own right.
But in *Stephen Hero* and the *Portrait* he adapted several into fuller contexts, so
from one point of view such 'epiphanies' have come to resemble a novelist's
jottings, the seeds of more substantial fiction. Here is one Joyce adapted for the
opening section of the *Portrait*.

(Bray: in the parlour of
the house in Martello Terrace).
Mr Vance—(comes in with a stick) . . . O, you know, he'll have to apologise,
Mrs Joyce.
Mrs Joyce—O yes . . . Do you hear that, Jim?
Mr Vance—Or else . . . if he doesn't the eagles'll come and pull out his eyes.
Mrs Joyce—O, but I'm sure he will apologise.
Joyce—(under the table to himself)
    —Pull out his eyes,
    Apologise,
    Apologise,
    Pull out his eyes.
    Apologise,
    Pull out his eyes,
    Pull out his eyes,
    Apologise.[3]

[1] Morris Beja, *Epiphany in the Modern Novel*, Peter Owen, 1971, pp. 71–2.

[2] The survivors have been published in R. Scholes and R. M. Kain, *The Workshop of Daedalus*, 1965.

[3] Chester G. Anderson (ed.), *James Joyce: A Portrait of the Artist as a Young Man*, Viking Press, 1968,
pp. 267–8.

This incident is dated between 1887 and 1891, and the 'epiphany' written down in 1901 or 1902. We'll look at some of the differences between it and the *Portrait* version shortly.

2.4 But what is an 'epiphany', and what is its bearing on Joyce's methods as a novelist? The account in *Stephen Hero* tells us a good deal. The incident is 'a triviality', yet it makes a deep impression on the observer. It is 'a sudden spiritual manifestation', a flash of significance, yet also 'delicate', 'evanescent'. In other words, its objective existence is unremarkable, and its importance lies in the meaning the novelist finds in it. What is this meaning? In most cases, it remains implicit, and even obscure. Look again at the extract from *Stephen Hero*. What does the snatch of dialogue *mean*? Without the introductory remark about 'Irish paralysis' it would be hard to say, and even with it, it is not easy. One effect is, I think, to stimulate the reader's imagination, to prompt him to invent a situation where such a conversation might provide a clinching— a revelatory—moment. The language, rhythms, tones of voice are specific, meticulously observed, condensed, suggesting definite traits in the speakers. Yet, in the end, quite what *is* being 'shown-forth' remains elusive.

2.5 The role of 'epiphanies' in Joyce's fiction has been widely commented on by Joyce's critics. Some propose that each *Dubliners* story is a distinct 'epiphany' of Dublin's paralysis, that each chapter of the *Portrait* ends in an 'epiphany' of Stephen's artistic development at that point, and that 'epiphanies' control the structure of *Ulysses*. But others think the whole emphasis overrated. (Joyce's wife seemed to take that view. Joyce records that 'when she saw me copy Epiphanies into my novel she asked would all that paper be wasted' (Beja, p. 84 n.).) The problem often is to decide where an 'epiphany' begins, because the revelatory effect is so dependent on the surrounding fictional context. Joyce often constructs his narratives—a term perhaps too traditional? —out of a succession of details, several of which could claim to be an 'epiphany' and whose impact is necessarily cumulative, so that if the last detail is the real 'epiphany' the reason could seem to lie in its *being* the last, rather than in some inherent quality. Yet the underlying idea of an apparently trivial gesture, event, conversation, description, being suddenly charged with significance, suddenly standing away from its context as *the* revealing episode, is a valuable clue in reading Joyce, certainly the earlier work, so deliberately implicit, deadpan, stripped of the novelist's usual pointers to 'meaning'.

2.6 **Exercise**

Perhaps a comparison between the original 'epiphany' quoted above, and its final version in the *Portrait* will be helpful. Read the first episode in the *Portrait*, Chapter 1, as far as '. . . Apologize' (Levin, pp. 52–3). What changes has Joyce made in adapting the 'epiphany'? What can you say about their relation to the rest of the chapter?

🙊🙊🙊🙊🙊🙊🙊🙊🙊🙊🙊🙊🙊🙊🙊🙊🙊🙊🙊🙊🙊🙊🙊🙊🙊🙊🙊🙊🙊🙊🙊🙊🙊🙊🙊

2.7 **Discussion**

The changes are clear enough.

(a) The original 'epiphany' now has a narrative context, a motive.

> The Vances lived in number seven. They had a different father and mother. They were Eileen's father and mother. *When they were grown up he was going to marry Eileen*. He hid under the table . . .
>
> Levin, p. 53, my italics

Stephen has been rude (sexually assertive?). The hiding under the table, the fierce threat, the little poem, are the results.

(b) Mr Vance's demand for an apology, and remark about the eagles, have now been divided between Stephen's mother and Dante.

(c) We are not explicitly told that Stephen speaks the verse because the novel is presented through his consciousness.

The first two changes clearly connect the episode with the rest of the chapter. Dante figures at the end of the next two sections, first as an Irish Nationalist and follower of Parnell, then as a supporter of the Church who condemned Parnell for a sexual offence; while in the fourth section, the Church punishes a number of boys for sexual offences, and Stephen successfully appeals against its unjust exercise of authority in the beating he received for having accidentally broken his glasses. (Note the reappearance of the point about eyes.) Stephen's mother is associated with Dante here because Joyce thought the power of the Church rested on the support it was given by women. In the third section the fiercest attacker of Parnell is an old woman. Later in the novel, we learn that religion, nationality, and the family are the threats to Stephen's growth as an artist (Levin, p. 247, and his first major rebellion is against the asceticism of the Church. Dante's threat to Stephen, then, prefigures the main themes of the novel. The third change brings Stephen's consciousness to the fore, the mocking little rhyme is his *artistic* response to Dante's threat, catching the child's feeling about the monotony of authoritative adults, with their rules and pre-scriptions. So, the sense in which the episode *is* an 'epiphany', and not just one of a group of childhood memories, lies in its relations with what follows. We can't really grasp its meaning except in the context of Stephen's develop-ment. Yet when we do, we can see why the first section moves towards this conclusion. The section records Stephen's early memories which mainly turn on his first relations with parents and related adults. It ends in one of them uttering a ferocious threat, and in Stephen making a defiant rhyme about it. The episode is an 'epiphany' of Stephen as an artist.

2.8 **Exercise**

You might find it useful to look at the conclusion of each of the other three sections in Chapter 1 of the *Portrait*, and decide whether they are 'epiphanies', if so what they amount to, and how they're related to each other. Make brief notes before going further.

2.9 **Discussion**

(a) Stephen having imagined his own death now has a dream about the death of Parnell. This establishes his self-identification with the nationalist hero. The episode seems to be an 'epiphany' of the theme of freedom, perhaps of what Ireland does to those who fight for it. (Later Stephen says to a patriotic student: 'No honourable and sincere man . . . has given up to you his life and his youth and his affections from the days of Tone to those of Parnell, but you sold him to the enemy or failed him in need or reviled him and left him for another . . . Ireland is the old sow that eats her farrow.' (Levin, pp. 211–12).)

(b) The end of the Christmas dinner party doesn't seem to me an 'epiphany' in the sense we've established, so much as a final dramatic gesture in an im-passioned scene. But this second emphasis on Parnell clearly matters. Notice also that it is the men, Mr Casey and Stephen's father, who mourn him—

Freedom = Parnell = Men versus Authority = Church = women seems to be the pattern emerging here.

(c) The ending of the fourth section illustrates the problem of where an 'epiphany' begins. The dramatic, or narrative, conclusion is Stephen being cheered by his schoolfellows for having struck a blow for freedom from arbitrary authority, followed by his own solitary—and improving—moral reflections: the Church clearly keeps its hold. The last two paragraphs, however, are different. Is this an 'epiphany', indirectly articulating a mood of peace and harmony?

> The air was soft and grey and mild and evening was coming . . . The fellows were practising long shies and bowling lobs and slow twisters. In the soft grey silence he could hear the bump of the balls: and from here and from there through the quiet air the sound of the cricket bats: pick, pack, pock, puck: like drops of water in a fountain falling softly in the brimming bowl.
>
> Levin, p. 95

Perhaps, yet the method seems little different from that of any novelist who registers feeling and mood with the help of descriptions. Remember the end of *Wuthering Heights*, or *Great Expectations*? If there is an 'epiphany', perhaps it is the whole page? But whatever we call it, the deliberate, structured beauty of the ending shouldn't be missed.

Taking all four endings together, there's a clear pattern. First, the child Stephen reacts against authority by composing a verse; then at Clongowes, ill because he refused to give in to a bully, he has a dream-identification with Parnell, a hero of Irish nationalism; next at home, the moral and political implications of the Church's denunciation of Parnell are brought out; and finally, Stephen's first blow for his own freedom from the Church is celebrated with a lyrical image of free, peaceful activity. I think this shows the value of the 'epiphany' approach to the *Portrait*, even if some uncertainty remains about specific cases.

2.10 Though none of the surviving originals has a place in them, the 'epiphany' is equally important in the *Dubliners* stories. Joyce wrote to a friend about his initial scheme: 'I call the series *Dubliners* to betray the soul of that hemiplegia or paralysis which many consider a city.' (*Letters*, I, 5.) He presents his characters and situations with the meticulous and economic realism of speech and gesture illustrated in the 'epiphany' in *Stephen Hero*. He builds the stories up from a series of incidents, of minimal *narrative* interest, towards a culminating remark or episode intended to crystallize the particular aspect of Dublin's paralysis which the story explores. In Joyce's letter, the word 'betray' is worth dwelling on. His characters *give themselves away* in details of behaviour, apparently trivial, but full of meaning for the observing, ironic novelist. This kind of 'epiphany' seems rather simpler than those we've looked at in the *Portrait*, where 'epiphanic' episodes have a more complexly expressive function, carrying the burden of major themes. The point is relevant to 'The Dead', where the final 'epiphany' of Gabriel's vision of the dead seems of a different order to those in earlier stories in the volume. Thus, one critic selects for its resemblance to the *Stephen Hero* 'epiphany' this conversation from 'Araby' which the boy of the story overhears.[1]

---

[1] Peter K. Garrett (ed.), *Twentieth Century Interpretations of 'Dubliners'*, Prentice-Hall, 1968, p. 12.

'—O, I never said such a thing?
—O, but you did!
—O, but I didn't!
—Didn't she say that?
—Yes, I heard her.
—O, there's a . . . fib!'

Levin, p. 373

The conversation 'betrays' the coy inanity of the flirtation, and leads the boy who overhears it to a recognition of the pointlessness of his own romantic dreams. This satirical function seems hardly the role of 'epiphanies' in 'The Dead'—for example, Gabriel's final vision of the snow falling all over Ireland —or in *The Portrait*.

There's a point of chronology to be remembered here. The *Stephen Hero* 'epiphany' is roughly contemporary with the early *Dubliners* stories, and Joyce's letter about the 'paralysis' theme. But 'The Dead' was written some years later, shortly before Joyce began the drastic revision of *Stephen Hero* which produced *The Portrait*, when, that is, his conception of fiction had already changed from the early ironic realism, and was changing again in the direction of *Ulysses*. There, too, moments of revelation are important. I would suggest that the brief episode we looked at (para. 1.17 (b)) when Dignam's coffin is lowered into the grave is an 'epiphany'. Suddenly, a new feeling emerges with telling power: not mourning, so much as shared and accepted sorrow at the common human fate. Again, though, I'm not convinced that we need a special critical term for this kind of thing. The important point is to recognize the kind of narrative pace and structure that depends for its deeper meanings on such moments.

2.11 Realism

Joyce began his literary career as a practitioner of 'realism'. He attacked the prevailing masters of the Irish Literary Movement because they failed to write about *real* Irish life. They wrote about their dreams, about idealised country peasants, about an imaginary, and in any case, a vanished heroic past. Joyce wrote about what he could see and hear, about the actual inhabitants of the city of Dublin, about the present. In *Stephen Hero* he says that:

Nearly every day Stephen wandered through the slums watching the sordid lives of the inhabitants. He read all the street ballads which were stuck in the dusty windows of the Liberties. He read the racing names and prices scrawled in blue pencil outside the dingy tobacco-shops, the windows of which were adorned with scarlet police journals. . . . He often posted himself opposite one of the factories in old Dublin at two o'clock to watch the hands coming out to dinner—principally young boys and girls with colourless, expressionless faces, who seized the opportunity to be gallant in their way. He drifted in and out of interminable chapels in which an old man dozed on a bench or a clerk dusted the woodwork or an old woman prayed before the candles she had lighted.

Stephen Hero, p. 129

Notice the attitude here. These are 'sordid' lives, inspected by the wandering observer, yet not unsympathetically: 'he *drifted* in and out of interminable chapels.' The scene, the people, have a kind of fascination. And this, mainly, is the spirit of *Dubliners*, a critical realism, emphasising its seamy side, yet sufficiently drawn by it to watch, to document, to remember.

Accuracy of detail was all important to Joyce. Writing about Dublin from Trieste, he would fire off questions to friends at home about points of detail: street-numbers, signs, names, advertisements, distances. The best-known case concerns the home of Mr Bloom at 7 Eccles Street, Dublin. Getting home late, and finding he'd lost his key, Bloom is said to climb over the railing and drop down into 'the area' to enter by the basement door. From Paris, Joyce wrote to his aunt to find out whether the height of the railing, and from the pavement to the area, were such that a man could actually do this.

2.12   Today, this kind of 'realism' seems normal, and even in Joyce's day, it had a tradition behind it. A strong impulse towards 'realism' belongs to the history of the Novel—a determination to give a true account of actuality, rather than 'romance'. Joyce also inherited the more immediate influence of the 'naturalist' movement emanating from France, and associated with Flaubert and Zola. And like the latter, his work was criticized, at least from the point of view of current taste, because its 'realism' offended the proprieties. We've seen how Edward Garnett felt the conventional reader would react to *The Portrait*. *Ulysses* met a similar fate for its frankness about the bodily functions. The French novelists Edmond and Jules Goncourt had said:

There is now only one consuming interest left in our life, the passion for living reality. Apart from that there is nothing but boredom and emptiness.[1]

[1] Ellman, R. and Feidelson, C., *The Modern Tradition*, O.U.P., 1965, p. 297.

Joyce would have concurred.

2.13 But as the discussion of 'epiphany' indicates, truthful observation is not enough to account for Joyce's methods. Indeed, the very notion of 'observer' is not simple. In *Dubliners*, Joyce's point of view is ostensibly that of a *neutral* observer, who does no more than document what he sees, confident that meticulous accuracy to the facts will carry their meaning. Yet clearly by 'epiphany' he intends the revelation of some special meaning, discovered by *him*, conveyed by *his* skill with words. A story like 'Eveline' is largely accounted for by 'realism', but with the 'The Dead' clearly this is not the case. As we move towards the story's climax, the documentary realism governing the presentation of the party gives way to more complex methods, different sorts of meaning, a peculiarly Joycean insight. To put the point more generally, as long as 'realism' involves laying bare what has been concealed from shame, ignorance, sentimentality, or fear, the novelist's task *is* largely documentary. The meaning of what he has to say exists in the tearing down of pretences. But beyond that essentially negative and critical task, there lies the more difficult one of positive

7 Eccles Street, Dublin
(*Noel Moffett*)

definition. 'Realism' as a method will hardly convey any novelist's particular vision of 'reality'. So we find Joyce moving away from the method of *Dubliners* through *The Portrait*, and into *Ulysses*, as he learned to master *his* sense of 'reality'.

2.14 Apart from 'epiphanies', what other methods did he develop? It's not possible to say much about this on the basis of our selective reading, but two points can, I think, be touched on. In both *The Portrait* and *Ulysses*, Joyce uses a combination of a narrator, and an individual consciousness, playing them off against each other to achieve effects a good deal more complex than either could create alone. In *The Portrait*, the unannounced shift from objective narration to Stephen's individual sense of the world has the effect of *objectifying* his experiences and judgements. Joyce was not implying a solipsistic world in which only Stephen's rendering of reality was real. But he does imply that only Stephen's attitudes really matter. The rest of the world matters only for what it reveals of Stephen. This gives the rendering of Stephen's experience memorable clarity and power, but it also involves significant ambiguities whenever the reader feels inclined to question Stephen's judgements. We can't see round Stephen. He remains, at certain, points, shadowy, as if Joyce himself can't make up his mind how to take him.

But in *Ulysses*, the more varied relation between the world presented by the narrator, and as experienced by Bloom, has the effect of enriching both. Bloom's judgements and interpretations are his, not his author's. Yet his intense and intelligent interest in the world about him co-operates with the narrator's objective presentation. Dublin exists in *Ulysses* not just because the narrator says it does, but pre-eminently because Bloom lives in it, and registers its impact as a feeling, observing, judging human being. The critic Auerbach linked Joyce with Virginia Woolf as examples of peculiarly modern writers for their use of 'multipersonal representation of consciousness'.[1] They had found a fictional method for giving a truer account of reality through a number of subjective impressions of it. In *Ulysses*, this happens through the intermingling of Stephen's, Bloom's and Mollie's ways of registering experience. I think we can add to that the flexible and subtle combination of narrator and individual consciousness—sometimes contrasting Bloom with a world that he feels alienated by, sometimes standing away from him in comic detachment, sometimes endorsing his deeper feelings and judgements. The narrator voices Joyce's consciousness, which transcends that of his characters, remains unobtrusive enough (there is no moralizing, or pointing of significances), but is not 'impersonal' in the *Dubliners* sense of pretending to have no point of view.

2.15 The other method is Joyce's use of myth to achieve generality of reference without losing the advantages of the specific 'realistic' surface. Take this paragraph, for example:

The high railings of Prospects rippled past their gaze. Dark poplars, rare white forms. Forms more frequent, white shapes thronged amid the trees, white forms and fragments streaming by mutely, sustaining vain gestures on the air.

Levin, p. 27

What is being referred to? Would you describe the method as 'realistic'? If not, how would you describe it? Do you see any evidence of the Greek myth, related by Homer, which Joyce used in 'Hades'? (Re-read my brief account of it in 1.16.)

[1] *Mimesis, The Representation of Reality in Western Literature*, 1968, Princeton University Press, p. 536.

The mourners are driving through Glasnevin Cemetery, but the method is not at all 'realistic'. I'm not sure there's any single name to describe it. 'Poetic'? 'Symbolic'? In reality, the white shapes and forms are the headstones of graves, glimpsed between the poplars as they drive past. But Joyce's marvellous control of rhythm, and use of devices of language we associate more with poems— the overtly musical quality, the metaphorical force of 'thronged', and 'mutely', suggesting a crowd of silent appealing ghosts—converts the scene into a modern version of an underworld peopled by the shades of the dead, and this is where the Greek myth comes in. Clearly the narrator here is far from neutral, or impersonal. He does much more than describe. He conveys the pathos and emptiness of the dead with eloquent sympathy. He announces, indirectly, that elegiac tenderness for the fact of death that Bloom voices on several occasions. A real scene, poetic methods, and reference to the Greek myth co-operate here to make a general statement about human experience central to the whole section. And so with characterization and narrative. On the surface, Bloom is a Dubliner of no special importance, but the parallel with Ulysses invites us to see him as hero of his times, a wanderer, maintaining certain values in an unsympathetic, sometimes a hostile world; while the story of 'Hades', on the surface a fragmentary account of a funeral, takes on shape and structure from the parallel with Homer: Odysseus' visit to the underworld; and this in its turn, carries Joyce's inner theme.

2.16 There's one further aspect of Joyce's 'realism' to mention—though at some risk of labouring the obvious—the use of the 'monologue intérieur' to dig more deeply into the roots of human personality, to include more about personal life, and to convey the sense of actually living from moment to moment. I expect you'll have had some thoughts about this kind of characterization compared with that of nineteenth-century novelists. So I'll postpone further comment till Section 3.

2.17 The Artist as Priest

Exercise

Here is an extract from *Stephen Hero*. Read it carefully, then jot down briefly what you think Jane Austen, Dickens, or George Eliot would have made of it.

The truth is not that the artist requires a document of licence from householders entitling him to proceed in this or that fashion but that every age must look for its sanction to its poets and philosophers. The poet is the intense centre of the life of his age. . . . He alone is capable of absorbing in himself the life that surrounds him or flinging it abroad again amid planetary music. When the poetic phenomenon is signalled to the heavens . . . it is time for (the critics) to acknowledge that here the imagination has contemplated intensely the truth of the being of the visible world and that beauty, the splendour of truth has been born.

Stephen Hero, pp. 67–8

2.18 **Discussion**

What would Jane Austen have said? Something, I'd guess, drily dismissive of the extravagant tone, firmly opposed to the notion that 'the poet is the intense centre of the life of his age'. Perhaps you remember Scott's praise of *Emma*:

The narrative of all her novels is composed of such occurrences as may have fallen under the observation of most folks; and her dramatis personae conduct themselves upon the motives and principles which the readers may recognize as ruling their own and that of most of their acquaintances. *The kind of moral, also, which these novels inculcate, applies equally to the paths of common life. . . .*

Novelists on the Novel, p. 66, my italics

Joyce's notion of radical opposition between 'householders' and 'artist' would probably have seemed meaningless to her, if not alarmingly subversive of her central beliefs.

Dickens, though thinking of a different *kind* of 'householder' from Jane Austen, would have been equally opposed to Joyce's view. Perhaps, though, he'd have been more sympathetic to the conclusion. He approved of fantasy, the artist's freedom to transform reality, but as a way of *responding* to his readers.

I have an idea (really founded on the love of what I profess) that the very holding of popular literature through a kind of popular dark age, may depend on such *fanciful* treatment.

op. cit, p. 66, my italics.

That falls far short of Joyce's ringing claim that the artist brings beauty into existence.

George Eliot would have been more likely to agree on that point. Ladislaw remarks:

To be a poet is to have . . . a soul in which knowledge passes instantaneously into feeling, and feeling flashes back as a new organ of knowledge. One may have that condition by fits only.

Middlemarch, p. 256

Would she have warmed to Joyce's assertion that the artist had no business with the attitudes of ordinary 'householders'? She would at least have understood it. She is sympathetic to the values of her provincial Middlemarchers, but also detached. As narrator, she *stands away* from her account of reality, putting always another point of view about *Middlemarch* than *Middlemarch* itself con-

38

tains. She is the first of our English novelists to claim for some of her characters (Dorothea, Lydgate, Ladislaw) special qualities of mind, imagination and feeling, which divide them from their society. Yet, in the end, she's equally concerned to affirm *common* values, that her novel may bridge the gap between the Dorotheas of life and the rest of us.

2.19 It's a deeply interesting issue, the writer's conception of his relation with society, and if you have time to explore the point further, look up *Novelists on the Novel*, p. 131, for a comment of Tolstoy's; *Cousin Bette*, pp. 214–16, for Balzac's view of the artist; and re-read Unit 23, Section II, especially the discussion of George Eliot and Henry James. What I wanted to bring out here is how uncompromising is Joyce's position. For him, *the artist and nobody else*, knows what 'life' is, and *his* imaginative response to it is the source of new truth and beauty. Other people's business is to *acknowledge* what the artist alone can reveal. No nineteenth century novelist says anything like that. But is it, as a point of view, entirely unfamiliar? Look again at Joyce's comment. Is he talking about *novelists*?

And read one more quotation:

Poets, according to the circumstances of the age and nation in which they appeared, were called, in the earlier epochs of the world, legislators, or prophets: a poet essentially comprises and unites both these characters. For he not only beholds intensely the present as it is . . . he beholds the future in the present, and his thoughts are the germs of the flower and the fruit of latest time.

If you happened to take *The Age of Revolutions* course (A202) you may recognize that as a quotation from Shelley's *A Defence of Poetry*.[1] Joyce's definitions also deal with 'poet', and 'artist', and like Shelley, like the poets of the Romantic period, claim for him the power of revelation.[2] The Romantic artist is a seer, a discoverer and creator of value. Joyce begins his career in that tradition, and though he moves away from the tone of Stephen's language, the basic idea remains. (It's an idea, incidentally, that continues to feed all avant-garde experimental art.) For Joyce, it was the business of the reader to follow him, never his to accommodate with his readers. Pre-eminently in Joyce's career, the Romantic definition of the *poet* seems to be at work, a reminder, amongst other implications that the conventional distinction between 'poet' and 'novelist' hardly applies to the concrete problems of the creative writer. You might like to consider at this point how far he's alone in this respect, how far other early twentieth-century novelists in the course share his position.

2.20 But this section is called 'The Artist as Priest'. Why? Chapter Five of *The Portrait of the Artist*, brings Stephen to the point just before he leaves Ireland and sets out on his artistic mission. It follows his rejection of the Church and first experience of creative inspiration, and is mainly filled by the account of his aesthetic ideas, and why they lead to his departure. In a brief episode he writes a poem to a girl who's been flirting both with him and with a priest. Attracted by her, he also despises her.

[1] *English Critical Essays* (Nineteenth Century), Oxford University Press, pp. 105–6.

[2] S. L. Goldberg, *The Classical Temper*, Chatto & Windus, 1963, pp. 59, 60.

His anger against her found vent in coarse railing at her paramour, whose name and voice and features offended his baffled pride: a priested peasant, with a brother a policeman in Dublin and a brother a potboy in Moycullen. To him she would unveil her soul's shy nakedness, to one who was but schooled in the discharging of a formal rite rather than to him, *a priest of the eternal imagination, transmuting the daily bread of experience into the radiant body of everliving life.*

Levin, p. 226, my italics.

Notice how thorough is the analogy with the priest, involving both the confessional and the rite of the eucharist. This conception of the artist-as-priest is Joyce's individual formulation of his Romantic inheritance. And it's interesting in two ways. First, as in the notion of 'epiphany', it shows how Joyce takes over for his own use a concept from the religion he'd abandoned as false. He gives a secular, this-worldly, content to a religious, other-worldly notion. Secondly, Shelleyan Romanticism refers extensively to 'the ideal', to a notion of reality that lies behind or within actual appearances. But for Joyce reality lay in the here and now. His idea is more like Wordsworth's, an irradiation of the commonplace, of the immediate stuff of experience, with his own particular vision. Yet it does continue to insist on the separate and special position of the artist. The artist reveals. The reader accepts the revelation as a kind of miracle. It also commits the artist to a peculiar kind of dedication, so that experience matters because it feeds his art. Experience is taken over into the work of art, and *transmuted*. It is the art that gives it meaning. One result of this is, as I expect you've realized, the peculiar place of 'epiphanies' in Joyce's art, special moments of insight, which both make sense of, and also transcend ordinary mundane happenings. Another is, I think, the character of Mr Bloom, not perhaps a 'priest of the eternal imagination', but gifted with the artist's ability to rescue the commonplace from oblivion, and isolated as a result.

It is the *isolation* that I think we need to notice in *The Portrait*. Stephen dedicates his creative gifts to the celebration of life, and that's a fair symbol of the spirit of Joyce's art. But it's life as observed, revealed, selected, by Joyce— *from a certain distance*. The artist-priest seems to share the experiences of the world he creates more fully than the world of common experience.

2.21 At the end of Section One, I asked you to make preliminary notes on ways Joyce differed from his nineteenth-century predecessors. Section Two will, I hope, have prompted further thoughts on the point, and before going on to Section Three, look again at what you said, adding to it in any appropriate way, and moving towards a view of the main question of the whole unit: what light does Joyce's kind of fiction throw on the achievements of the previous century? where does he extend them in a natural development? and where does he break radically new ground?

3.0 SECTION THREE

3.1 There's the usual difficulty at this point of not being able directly to discuss the subject with you. I don't know what issues you've thought important, but my own suggestions here will certainly be of little use unless you've already ventilated some of these points in connection with your own reading. Early in the course, some students commented in the 'feedback' on how irritating it was when course unit authors said again and again that their own remarks weren't authoritative, and that students could make up their own mind. A fair point. But it is still necessary to keep saying that unless you do your own thinking, what you read in the units is all too likely to be absorbed in an uncritical way. Another 'feedback' comment was that despite the attempt at debate within each unit, the effect of reading them was too much like arguing with a brick wall. Precisely. That's the danger we all feel, and especially when it comes to conclusions like this. So, let me repeat, if you haven't done some preliminary note-taking on the points I raised at the end of Sections One and Two, it would be wiser not to read any more of the unit.

Here are my comments, in note form, to underline their tentativeness.

3.2 Story, Plot

Very little in J. Think of Balzac, Dickens, George Eliot—complication, surprise, suspense, strong forward movement. 'Eveline': two moments only, one with her sitting, remembering; the second, her unexplained refusal to go abroad. 'The Dead': rambling, episodic, vaguely chronological movement; things happen, rather than are narrated. *The Portrait*: story-line provided by chronology of growing up, but again no sense of excitement, or looking-forward, but a succession of 'significant' events, unlinked by anything you might call 'plot'. *Ulysses*: funeral ceremony provides story, such as it is, and in novel, the succession of hours. But there is, also, the 'inner story'—Bloom as a modern Ulysses, adventuring abroad. Taken over from Homer, though.

Why? connection with J's 'realism'? Stories impose a false pattern on experience which is fragmented, episodic, an endless flow? Some deep issues here: (a) 'stories' move towards a conclusion, in serious novelists this implies aims and purposes. End of *Great Expectations* expresses D's view of what finally happened to Pip as result of his mistakes. End of *Mansfield Park, Middlemarch*, show novelist's sense of values, what accomplishments she approves and disapproves. J's values not expressed that way? Accomplishment is 'inner', to do with reflections on life (Gabriel, Bloom), not with achievement. (b) Also, purposive action takes place in time. J's notion of routine of a single day enclosing all significant life implies pointlessness of action in time. Nothing to achieve accept survival.

3.3 Characterization

Deeper than nineteenth century? Hardly in *Dubliners*. Gabriel Conroy presented more intimately, but not more deeply than, say, Hardy's Jude. But *Portrait* quite different from handling of Fanny, Pip, Maisie: probes into earlier stage of life, conceives consciousness differently, perceptions, feelings, not just thoughts; traces Stephen's mental-emotional development in new detail, and understanding. Same freshness in Bloom's varied responses to experience, but here seems more an extension of exploration of adult consciousness begun in previous century. Certain taboos have dissolved (been destroyed?), certain proprieties have gone. But this already shows in Hardy? More radical change is direct presentation of Bloom's mind in act of observing, reflecting, interpreting: its energy, resilience, penetration, imaginative life. Nothing quite like this in nineteenth century

3.4 Structure

In the nineteenth century, 'structure' usually provided by story or plot. J, builds by assembling episodes with faintest of story-lines, but in significant thematic connection. 'The Dead': Gabriel's wife listening to song, his aesthetic response

41

to her, contrasted with his final view in hotel—illusion followed by reality. In 'Hades', events prompt Bloom to series of reflections which add up to critical probing of attitudes towards death. Thematic pattern the key to structure, underlined by reference to Homer myth. Theme, in nineteenth century, matters, but less obtrusive, because combined with, or expressed by, story-line. James cuts from episode to episode insisting on Maisie's situation but her story still holds attention. So more markedly, with Dickens and G. Eliot. 'Structure' in J tailored to express vision of life: movement of 'The Dead' to Gabriel's final thoughts; *Ulysses* intermingles Stephen's, Bloom's and Molly's sense of reality. Also reflects powerful artistic discipline. Sense of 'this book has been *made* by J', rather than 'this story has been told . . .'

3.5 Language

Language always matters, but much *more* significant in J. Without careful attention to it, work hardly meaningful, whereas plenty to be got from Dickens, and Eliot without looking closely at language. J is more packed, carefully worked, more allusive. Success of 'epiphanies' depends wholly on quality of language. Changes in Stephen's infant mind, active energy of Bloom's, depend entirely on effects of language, crucial interplay of narrator and Bloom reflected in different language styles. Sensitive and brilliant use of 'poetic' devices, imagistic, rhythmical—to create these effects. Bloom's meditations have implicit form, not unlike poems, conveyed by subtle shifts of mood and attitude through language effects. *Stephen Hero*: J has Stephen theorizing about 'the poet'. Right term for author of *Ulysses*?

3.6 Other points

A reminder that if you haven't covered them in your notes on the main headings, two major points came up in Section Two. One is Joyce's more complex conception of 'realism', gradually worked towards from *Dubliners* to *Ulysses*. Nineteenth-century novelists assume there *is* a real world, acknowledged and understood by writer and reader alike, with which the invented world of his novel has a simple correspondence. Joyce's view implies that everyone makes his own 'real world' out of the endless flux of experience. We all share life and its necessary appetites, and we all die, but beyond that there is no common structure of inhabited reality, but only 'happenings' into which we have greater or less insight. The other is Joyce's relation with his reader. I think this is a development of tendencies strongly affecting George Eliot and James, but the kind of development that amounts to a radical departure. Perhaps it can be put this way. Dickens assumes common ground with his readers, more or less comfortably. Eliot and James only assume common ground with certain kinds of reader: the implication is, that to understand them the reader has developed a special kind of insight into life, belonging only to the few. But Joyce expects nothing—and everything. He assumes no common ground, but insists that the reader join him on his: every reader his own (solitary) artist. Also, as his formidable artistic armoury suggests, he's more indifferent to his readers, who can easily choose to ignore him. But so much the worse for them, it makes no difference to Joyce. James, great and assured artist as he was, never aspired to that degree of self-confidence.

What do you think a novelist gains and/or loses by that sort of relation with his readers?

Further Reading

Joyce's work is the important 'further reading': I'd suggest plunging straight into *Ulysses*; but the rest of the *Dubliners* collection (e.g. 'A Painful Case', 'Ivy Day in the Committee Room', 'The Boarding House'), and of *The Portrait* are more immediately accessible. (All these titles are published by Penguin.) *Finnegans Wake*, on which Joyce spent the rest of his life after completing *Ulysses*, should be postponed for later reading, but you might try the extract in Levin.

Other reading

Richard Ellmann *James Joyce*, Oxford University Press, 1959. The definitive biography.

Harry Levin *James Joyce*, New Directions, 1960. A general introduction.

S. L. Goldberg *The Classical Temper*, Oxford University Press, 1961. A valuable work of criticism.

W. Y. Tindall *A Reader's Guide to James Joyce*, New York, 1959. A useful reference book for tracking Joyce's allusions.

Frank Budgen *James Joyce and the Making of Ulysses*, Oxford University Press, 1972. A straightforward account of the novel, interpolated with Budgen's memories of Joyce and his own occasional interpretations.

Stanislaus Joyce *My Brother's Keeper*, Faber, 1958. A memoir by Joyce's brother.

Stuart Gilbert, Richard Ellmann, *The Letters of James Joyce*, 3 vols., Faber, 1957–66.

Acknowledgements

Grateful acknowledgement is made to the following sources for material used in this unit:

The Bodley Head for James Joyce, *Ulysses;* Noel Moffett; National Library of Ireland; Southern Illinois University at Carbondale for the Croessman Collection of James Joyce; Phyllis Thompson; H. C. White Collection.

The Nineteenth-century Novel and its Legacy